Kid Wonder
and the
Half-Hearted
Hero

Stephen Elboz

Illustrated by Judy Brown

Chapter One

At Haddit House, home for retired superheroes, there was great excitement. A new gentleman called Mr Biggs was coming to live with them.

'*New*,' chuckled Grandpa. 'Don't you mean *old*?'

'A new old gentleman,' said Matron. 'He used to be the Black Lightning over at Omah City. But now he has retired and his grandson has taken his place as crime fighter.'

Grandpa smiled. It was just the same here at Baggem City. His granddaughter, Kid Wonder, had taken over as superhero.

Suddenly there was a crash of glass. A stranger stood in front of a broken window.

Matron frowned. 'Mr Biggs! Now you have retired, kindly use the door like everyone else.'

'So sorry,' said Mr Biggs. 'I keep forgetting I'm no longer a superhero.'

Mr Biggs looked a little lost, so Grandpa offered to show him around.

'Remember! Use the doors,' growled Matron, marching away.

Grandpa helped Mr Biggs to take his suitcase up to his room.

'It feels funny not having my super-strength any more,' said Mr Biggs sadly.

'Never mind, at least your grandson is carrying on with your crime-fighting work,' said Grandpa. 'What's your grandson's name now he's a superhero?'

'Well,' began Mr Biggs. 'I hoped he'd call himself Jet Junior, but he wants to be known as Doughnut Boy.'

'Doughnut Boy?' said Grandpa.

'He likes doughnuts,' explained Mr Biggs. 'He likes them a lot.'

'If he's as good at crime-fighting as my granddaughter, Kid Wonder,' said Grandpa proudly, 'then it doesn't matter what he's called.'

Suddenly Mr Biggs burst into tears.

'What's wrong?' asked Grandpa.

'The truth is,' said Mr Biggs, 'my grandson is a terrible superhero. Do you think Kid Wonder would give him lessons and teach him how to ⚡ZAP⚡ a few criminals?'

'I'm sure she would,' said Grandpa. 'I'll call her on the wonderphone straight away.'

Chapter Two

Kid Wonder flew to Haddit
House as soon as she got
Grandpa's call.

She liked Mr Biggs but she was not
too happy when she heard about his
grandson.

'Doughnut Boy!' she
cried when they told
her his name.

'He likes doughnuts,'
explained Mr Biggs.

'A lot,' said Grandpa.

Kid Wonder sighed. 'I suppose it
wouldn't hurt to give him a lesson or
two in fighting crime,' she said. 'Tell
him to meet me on the roof of City
Hall at ten o'clock tomorrow.'

The next day at ten o'clock, Kid Wonder landed on the roof of City Hall.

There was nobody else around, just a few sparrows. Kid Wonder looked at her wonderwatch… and kept on looking at it every few minutes.

At last she heard something.

Coming up the fire escape was a boy eating a bag of doughnuts.

'Doughnut Boy, you're late!' growled Kid Wonder.

'Sorry,' said Doughnut Boy. 'I had an emergency to deal with… I ran out of doughnuts.'

'Why did you use the fire escape instead of flying?' demanded Kid Wonder.

Doughnut Boy grinned. 'It's not my fault,' he said. 'I always get a belly-ache if I try to fly on a full stomach.'

Before Kid Wonder could say any more, she heard alarm bells. She ran to the side of the building and looked down. Aha! A crime was taking place.

Baby-face Brewster had just raided the Soft and Cuddly Toy Shop and stolen a teddy bear. He ran from the shop and leapt into his get-away pram.

'Go! Go!' he shouted at Squeaky Malloy, his getaway driver.

Kid Wonder turned quickly to Doughnut Boy. 'Here's your chance to go into action,' she said.

'Um... I'll just finish this last doughnut,' he said.

Kid Wonder sighed. She grabbed his cape, lifted him into the air and set him down in the street.

'Get to work, Doughnut Boy,' she ordered. 'Go and catch some villains!'

Doughnut Boy plodded off down the street.

'It's a superhero!' squealed Baby-face Brewster. 'Let's get out of here.'

'We'd better slow down a bit,' whispered Squeaky Malloy, 'or we might escape too easily.'

Doughnut Boy stopped for a rest.

Baby-face Brewster and Squeaky Malloy waited for him on a street corner. But what was this? Doughnut Boy had fallen asleep.

'That is *so* rude,' snarled Squeaky Malloy. 'We deserve to get treated properly.'

'Yes,' agreed Baby-face Brewster. 'It's criminal.'

Chapter Three

'Eh? What's wrong?' yawned Doughnut Boy as somebody shook him awake.

Kid Wonder stared hard at him. 'You let those criminals escape,' she said.

'Never mind,' smiled Doughnut Boy. 'I expect some more will come along in a minute.'

Sure enough, as he finished speaking, another alarm bell went off, and from a nearby jewellery shop raced the Slippery Shadow and Fingers O'Brien.

They each carried a bag of stolen loot.

'Off you go – and don't mess it up this time,' said Kid Wonder, giving Doughnut Boy a helpful shove.

'Hey... stop,' said Doughnut Boy weakly.

'A superhero!' gulped the Slippery Shadow. 'Let's get back to the hide-out, fast.'

The Slippery Shadow and Fingers O'Brien sped down the street. But when they looked back...

'In all my years as a criminal I have never been so insulted!' shouted the Slippery Shadow.

Fingers O'Brien nodded in agreement.

The Slippery Shadow threw down his bag of loot. 'I am going to call a special meeting of all the city's villains!' he roared.

That night, in a secret underground drain,

Sorry, my criminal mask is at the cleaners.

the Slippery Shadow stood on a chair to talk to the many criminals gathered there.

'Villains!' he began. 'Stealing is not what it used to be. In the old days, if you stole something, you were sure to be chased by a superhero. These days we are being ignored. Superheroes have turned soft. So what are we going to do about it?'

The villains muttered together for a moment.

'What *can* we do?' called a pickpocket at the back of the crowd.

The Slippery Shadow thought for a while. Then a cunning smile appeared on his face. 'We'll go on strike!' he said. 'There'll be no more crime in Baggem City until crime-fighters treat us with more respect.'

Then his smile grew wider and even more cunning. 'Believe me, we can have a lot of fun from this,' he said. And he told them his plan.

Chapter Four

That same night at City Hall, the Police Department was very quiet. Too quiet. The phones didn't ring and the cells stood empty.

The police had nothing to do but polish their handcuffs and draw silly things on the wanted posters.

Police Chief McGrabbem looked at the clock and yawned. What was going on?

The next morning, even stranger things began to happen. All over Baggem City, doorbells were being rung.

Burglars were handing back stolen property.

The Slippery Shadow watched and smiled to himself.

Meanwhile, down at City Hall, the Slippery Shadow had ordered other criminals to protest outside Police Chief McGrabbem's window.

Without crime, the newspapers had hardly anything to write about.

Like the police, Kid Wonder had nothing to do. Nothing except watch Doughnut Boy scoff doughnut after doughnut.

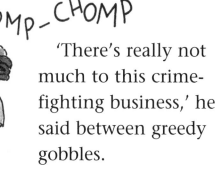

CHOMP-CHOMP

'There's really not much to this crime-fighting business,' he said between greedy gobbles.

Kid Wonder left him and decided to fly over the city again.

It was night time, the time criminals love best. If Kid Wonder was going to catch a wrong-doer, it was going to be now.

She was right.

Down below, she saw a burglar sneaking out of a window.

Kid Wonder swooped down and caught him red-handed.

'Hold it right there, you law-breaker!' she said.

'Gulp!' said the burglar.

No sooner had Kid Wonder grabbed him than she saw another burglar, and another, and another. They were all creeping out of houses up and down the street.

It was a crime wave!

Kid Wonder radioed Police Chief McGrabbem for help. Soon wailing police sirens could be heard all over the city, and the cells began filling up fast.

Whee-uu-Wheeuu-Wheeuu-

Chapter Five

Down at City Hall, Police Chief McGrabbem wiped his hot face with a handkerchief.

'What a night!' he said. 'I knew that Baggem City's criminals couldn't stay away from crime for too long. Let's go along to the cells and see who these villains are.'

'The Slippery Shadow and his gang are sure to be there,' said Kid Wonder.

She followed the Police Chief down some stone steps to the cells.

Hundreds of sad faces peered at them through the bars.

'Right, you criminals!' said the Police Chief. 'Time to take off your masks and show yourselves.'

All together, the criminals reached up and tugged at their masks.

When the masks came off, the Police Chief and Kid Wonder gasped in amazement.

'Why look!' whispered Police Chief McGrabbem. 'There's Mr and Mrs Henderson who live across the road from me, and Mr George who owns the pet shop where we buy our police dogs.'

'And there's Mrs Alfred my school teacher,' said Kid Wonder, pointing. 'And the vicar of St Ethelbert's church.'

'But you're just *ordinary* people,' said Police Chief McGrabbem. 'Why did you steal your own things?'

There was a long silence before anyone spoke.

In the end, Miss Tong the librarian stepped up to the bars.

'It's like this,' she began in her small librarian's voice. 'When a burglar brought back what he had stolen from me, I was worried about the neighbours. Perhaps they'd think that my things simply weren't good enough for a burglar to take. I worried about it so much that I decided to break into my own house and steal them myself.'

'And is that what you all did?' asked Kid Wonder.

Hundreds of guilty faces nodded in agreement.

'The Slippery Shadow helped us,' they all said. 'He gave us lessons on how to become burglars.'

'He even lent us our masks,' added Miss Tong.

Huh, I bet he did.

33

Police Chief McGrabbem scratched his head. 'This strike is turning the whole world upside down,' he said. 'It's making honest people act like villains, and villains act like honest people.'

'I expect that's just what the Slippery Shadow planned all the time,' said Kid Wonder. With that, she gave everyone there a stern warning and sent them home to bed.

Kid Wonder knew that she had to find the Slippery Shadow and sort things out before they got any worse.

Chapter Six

Kid Wonder flew back and forth over the city, calling out the Slippery Shadow's name. She carried a white flag to show that she meant no trouble.

At last a torch beam flashed at her, and when she flew down to check it out, a voice hissed through a half-opened door.

Kid Wonder gripped the white flag tightly and crept through the door. She found herself in a small den lit by a candle. Around the candle sat the Slippery Shadow and his gang. They looked very pleased with themselves.

'You can't arrest us, Kid Wonder,' hissed the Slippery Shadow at once. 'We've done nothing wrong.'

'That's the trouble,' said Kid Wonder. 'If you can't trust villains to be dishonest, who can you trust?'

They sat down on broken stools
and old boxes and began to talk. They
talked and talked. They talked all
through the night until at last they
reached an agreement.

The Slippery Shadow was pleased
at the trouble he was causing. But
he badly missed his life of crime,
and he agreed to call off the strike
if Doughnut Boy acted like a proper
superhero.

'He must treat us with the respect we
deserve,' added the Slippery Shadow.

He already had a plan. 'My gang will be robbing Baggem City Bank on Friday morning,' he said. 'Make sure that Doughnut Boy is there to try and stop us.'

Kid Wonder grinned. 'Don't worry. He'll be there.'

Chapter Seven

By Friday, news of the bank robbery had spread all over Baggem City.

Large crowds turned out to watch it, and there were newspaper reporters and TV crews.

When the Slippery Shadow and his gang saw so many people waiting for them, they turned around and dashed back to their hide-out... to change into their best clothes.

The Slippery Shadow put on some make-up so his face wouldn't look shiny when he was filmed.

The crowds cheered as the gang
raced back and dodged into the bank.

'Hold it there, everyone,' shouted
the Slippery Shadow. 'This is a – '

'Yes – yes, a stick
up,' said the bank
manager. 'We were
expecting you hours
ago. Now here's all
the money ready for
you. Is it enough? I'll
help you carry it to
the door.'

When the Slippery Shadow and his
gang took the money, all of the bank
staff clapped. The gang took a bow.

Outside on the street, you could almost feel the excitement. Everyone was waiting for Doughnut Boy to show up.

'Come on, we haven't got all day,' called the Slippery Shadow.

Then all at once he appeared.

DOUGHNUT BOY

He stood on a high roof-top looking down at the gang, his cape spread out like wings.

'Hooray!' shouted the crowds.

'Let's get away from here quite quickly,' said the Slippery Shadow.

'Not so fast,' boomed Doughnut Boy. 'I'm here to see that justice is done.'

'Oh, and what are you going to do, you great wet lettuce leaf?' sniggered Fingers O'Brien.

'This – '

The crowds gasped.

Doughnut Boy had leapt off the roof and was flying straight towards the gang like an angry wasp.

In the crowds, Grandpa and Mr Biggs watched proudly.

'Look! He's flying,' gasped Mr Biggs. 'He's flying like a proper superhero!'

In a way this was true.

The Slippery Shadow and his gang ducked as Doughnut Boy swished low over them.

'This superhero means business,' squeaked Squeaky Malloy.

'Do you know, I think he does,' said the Slippery Shadow.

They raced down the road as fast as they could, dropping stolen bank notes behind them.

Doughnut Boy flew up into the sky and landed on a tall skyscraper.

'Time for a doughnut,' he said.

'Oh, no!' groaned Kid Wonder. 'If he stops for a snack now, he'll lose the chase for good.'

Down below, the crowds groaned too. If Doughnut Boy didn't behave like a proper superhero, then the strike of villains would go on.

Doughnut Boy pulled an extra large doughnut from under his cape...

…and he threw it!

Other doughnuts came dropping from the sky behind it.

Before the Slippery Shadow and his gang knew what was happening, Doughnut Boy had landed and arrested them all.

'Well done, Doughnut Boy!' cried Police Chief McGrabbem.

A great roar went up from the crowds.

Doughnut Boy smiled proudly. Then he picked up the doughnuts… and ate them. He thought it would be a shame if they went to waste.

Chapter Eight

The strike of villains ended that very hour. Soon alarm bells were ringing merrily all over Baggem City, sounding as sweet as music to the Baggem City police force.

This time, whenever the law was broken, it was broken by a proper criminal.

We'll be along in a moment!

As the crowds went off to their homes, Police Chief McGrabbem had his pocket picked. He didn't really mind because things were at last back to normal.

Just then Kid Wonder zoomed down
from the sky. 'Have I missed
anything?' she asked innocently.

'You should have been here, Kid
Wonder,' cried Mr Biggs, doing a little
dance. 'Doughnut Boy is a hero.'

After a great fuss had been made of
Doughnut Boy, Grandpa turned to Kid
Wonder.

'Will you fly me back to Haddit
House?' he asked. 'I'm sure Doughnut
Boy would be happy to fly Mr Biggs
there too.'

'Er... it's such a lovely day, why don't
we walk there instead?' said Kid
Wonder. She winked at Doughnut Boy,
who grinned.

At Haddit House, Doughnut Boy got ready to go back to his own city to fight crime. Mr Biggs looked at him fondly.

'Just you make sure you don't fly in the rain,' he said. 'And always wear a warm vest and have a clean hanky every day...'

'Don't worry,' whispered Kid Wonder in Doughnut Boy's ear. 'All grandpas are like this – even grandpas of superheroes.'

Then it was time for Doughnut Boy
to leave.

'Wait for me,' said Kid Wonder. 'I'll
show you the best way to go. Here,
hold my hand. We can fly together.'

'Bye!' shouted Grandpa and Mr
Biggs.

They both waved madly as they
watched the two superheroes zoom up
into the sky.

When Kid Wonder had seen
Doughnut Boy safely aboard a bus, she
flew back to Haddit House. Grandpa
was alone in the garden.

He winked at her as she landed beside him. 'Clever you, Kid Wonder,' he said quietly. 'You made it look as if Doughnut Boy was flying all by himself.'

'You knew all the time?' cried Kid Wonder.

'Of course, I'm your Grandpa. You can't fool me.'

Kid Wonder slipped her arm through his. 'But Doughnut Boy has promised me he *will* practise his flying and do all the things a superhero does. He even promised to eat a few less doughnuts.'

Grandpa began to chuckle. 'If he sticks to the bit in the middle, then he can eat as many as he likes.'

fat free
no artificial colours
sugarless
no calories

'Oh, Grandpa,' laughed Kid Wonder. 'You *are* terrible at times.'

About the author

When I was growing up I had a very sweet tooth and it always seemed that chocolate bars were never quite big enough. So I had a plan. I was going to save up chocolate for several weeks, then scoff the lot in one glorious midnight feast. I bought a Mars bar and hid it under my bed – but after an hour I could stand it no longer... I just had to have it. So my greedy plan failed.

I expect some would say that's because I'm a lot like Doughnut Boy!